Dedicated to children everywhere

who do not know what they want to do…

yet.

Copyright©2018 Vickie Massey Witherspoon. All rights reserved.

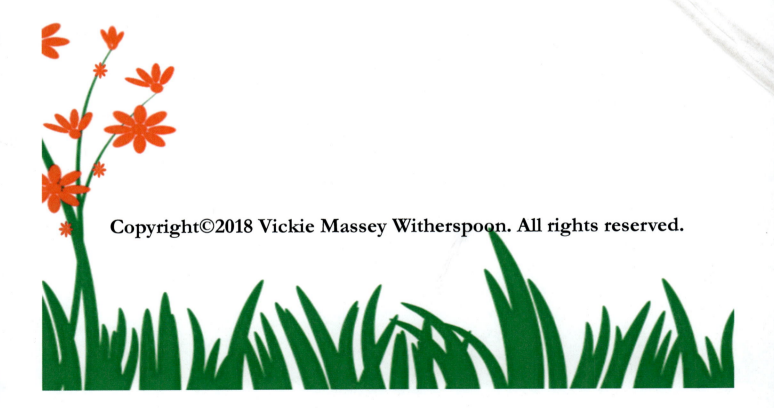

Pourquoi Tales

The concept of the book is to offer a story that tells why: a *pourquoi* tale. The premise is to select unusual animals, create an imaginative reason why they do the things they do or look the way they look, and incorporate a valuable life lesson in the tale. It is the author's hope that this is the first of a series of *pourquoi* tales.

Oxi Finds His Purpose

A Pourquoi Tale: Why Oxpeckers Peck

By Vickie Massey Witherspoon

Illustrated by Winter Broadhurst

Deep in the African jungle, the trees reach high toward the clear blue sky.

The plants and bushes are tall and thick, and greener than shiny emeralds.

The flowers are bright and brilliant—yellow, orange, and red.

They drape like canopies above our heads.

Big brown vines are found throughout, to help the monkeys get about,

And maybe a human if he's daring.

The sun's radiant rays dance in and out.

At times, we all cover our eyes because of its intense glaring.

A giant elephant comes into view, with a baby elephant holding on to its tail.

Then I spy a giraffe, and her new calf with necks longer than sailboats' sails.

Happy families are all around me. I look at my mate and smile. He says to me, as he looks at our eggs,

"Don't worry dear, our little ones will be here in a while."

Oh the joy that I feel knowing, that I will be a mother soon.

Daddy and I are excited beyond words, simply over the moon.

The Oxpecker family will soon be complete.

Big Oxi and I can hardly wait - for them to walk, fly, hunt on their own, and eventually find a mate.

We are expecting five little ones, all five I long to meet.

I long to see their feathers, beaks, and tiny little feet.

We have been preparing for a very long time. The nest is soft and thick, and Daddy Oxpecker has supplies stored up to feed the newborn chicks. What will they be? What will they do?

"As my mom told me, I now tell you,
'My love, there is a special job out there just for you, that only you will be able to do.
All in time, my love, in time.'"

I hear a rumble in the nest.
I watch the eggs gently moving about.
It won't be long - not long at all - until one by one,
all five babies will pop out.

Oh my, the first one's here! His feathers are brown and his beak is yellow.

He looks just like his dad.

Oh, what a charming fellow.

Now, baby two is making its grand entrance into the world.

Yes, thank God, it's a girl!

Two more come forth without a hitch,

but the last little

Oxpecker was having a bit of a glitch.

He stretched this way and then that way, and cracked the egg just a bit.

I just could not stand it anymore, and with my beak I gave the egg a gentle hit.

He is here, with a red beak and dark brown feathers
with a small green dot.
It sets him apart from the rest, and I like it
quite a lot.
Training started straightaway: to eat, to jump, to fly.
Before we knew it, they were all grown up.
Boy, how time did fly.
They all have good jobs: two guides, a guard, a vet.
But my last Oxpecker, Oxi,
doesn't know what he wants to do yet.

He said, "Mom,
what will I be? What will I do?
I want to be successful, too."
I looked at him and shared these words.
"What my mom told me, I now tell you,

*'My love, there is a special job out there just for you,
that only you will be able to do.
All in time, my love, in time.'"*

My special little Oxi was flying about the Wood,

when he heard a water buffalo moaning,

and it didn't sound very good.

Oxi went down and asked,

"What's wrong? What can I do to help out?"

The water buffalo replied,

"There are things on my back. They're crawling all about."

Oxi said, "I see them," as he started to peck and peck.

He did not leave a single bug, not a single speck.

Oxi remembered what I'd told him,

what my mom had always told me,

"My love, there is a special job out there just

for you, that only you will be able to do.

All in time, my love, in time."

The time had finally come
when **Oxi** had his special job to do.
He is now a well-known pecker,
and he is helping other animals too.
Water Buffalo told all his friends,
and they lined up one by one.
The impala, the giraffe, the rhino—
all loved the job he'd done.

The Oxpecker family is complete.

We have all found our place in life.

If I were to leave one profound thought to this universe

filled with toil and strife,

it would be - be yourself,

and don't worry about being like another.

Don't dare to compare yourself, even to a sister or a brother. Just know that in time, my love,

you will discover the job meant for you,

for there is one special job out there,

that only you can do.

The End...

No, Only The Beginning.

Jeremiah 29: 11

"For I know the plans I have for you, says the Lord. They are plans for good and not for evil, to give you a future and a hope."

Oxpeckers have what is called a symbiotic relationship with the animals they relieve. They help each other.

The oxpecker rids animals like the rhino, water buffalo, giraffe, or impala of parasites,

and the animals provide food for the oxpecker.

Photo by Derek Keats

Can you think of other animals that help each other?

About the Author

Vickie Massey Witherspoon is a South Carolina native and a mother of three. She started writing short stories and poetry in elementary school. She would like to thank God for giving her the gift of storytelling. She would also like to thank her family and friends for their support. She pays homage to her sixth grade teacher, Ms. Mackey for declaring she was a writer. She believed her.

About the Illustrator

Winter Broadhurst is a freelance artist, writer, and editor. She enjoys taking her and others' ideas and bringing them to life through artistic representations. Broadhurst primarily works with water colors, inks, and digital design. She would like to thank all those who supported her on this illustration journey and helped her find the inspiration to create.

Made in the USA
Monee, IL
15 March 2022

92954435R10017